In Queen Mary's Gardens

For Dave & Colette
The Man with the
magic fingers

Tom Morgan
14/11/91

Tom Morgan

Acknowledgements are due to the following magazines in which some of these poems first appeared: Force 10 (2 & 3); The Dundalk Magazine; The Sligo Champion; Gown, Fortnight.

Cover by Dan Dowling
Backcover photograph by Noel Kilgallon
Typeset & Design by Johan Hofsteenge
Printed by Colour Books, Dublin
Hardback Binding by Kenny's Fine Binding, Galway

The publisher acknowledges the financial assistance of the Arts Council of Northern Ireland in the publication of this volume.

© Tom Morgan 1991. All Rights Reserved.

ISBN 0 948339 80 2 Hardcover £8.50
ISBN 0 948339 81 0 Softcover £4.95

Salmon Publishing, The Bridge Mills, Galway, Ireland

For my family

Contents

Laganside	11
When The Order Came To Move	12
The Scud	13
Should Feel Like Home	14
The Hidden Curriculum	15
Under the Bridge	16
The Reservation	17
Marriage	18
In Queen Mary's Gardens	19
Mother	20
Shooting Stars at Ben Whisken	21
A Small Peace	22
The Cooler	23
Our Day Will Come	24
Echoes	25
Sean O'Riada in Belfast	26
Quilting in Ballintrillick	27
Pecking Order	28
Under the Glare of Blue	29
Walking the Dog	30
Gortnahowla	31
Summer Evening in the Gaeltacht	32
Belfast Wakes	33
In Monaghan	34
Annacuna	35

My Daughter Asleep	36
The Strangest Angle	37
Maisonette Madonna	38
Tobernalt	39
Both Taig an Prod	40
Driving the Roads of Sligo	41
With Hearts Cut Out	42
Ramblers	43
Joy-Riders	44
Ritual	45
Tooneenvalley	46
The Sonorous Streets	47
Not Today Son, Not Today	48

Laganside

The Lagan of silt and tins
shifts with the tide.
Over the murky weir
there's a leaden sky
and a cold rain.
A pram is stuck
in mud at its edge
and a woman stumbles,
stumbles and writhes.
The air is heavy with gloom;
a woman and her pram,
a flight of starlings
smoking oppressive skies.

When the Order Came to Move

Handy to water, mother snibbed the window back
and let the top half down; leaned outside with her
teapot, fed geraniums and weeds on the ground.

When the order came to move we packed the van
and headed for the newly-built estate which
sprawled in all directions below Divis Mountain.

Mother held the pots on her knee until she
laid them out on new sills to breath in the view.
They died later one Summer's day, their reds and greens
feeling her touch like dust under the shifting blue.

The Scud

She danders down the cracked pavement
past children kicking ball which flies
above her head to weeds in no mans' land.
One yells, 'Away til hell suck-the-butts.'
When she bends for stones her varicose veins are
visible through holes in grey-black socks.
At the army barracks soldiers reinforce with
wire and sheets of corrugated tin.
One shouts, 'Old Maggie suck-the-butts,' and
laughs. Another lifts his head and joins in.
She stops; picks a bit of grass and chews cud.
'Away til Saddie Arabia,' she yells, 'with yer
mates and tanks. Thon big darkie'll give yis scud.'

Should Feel Like Home

Night pours from eyes and haloed lamps flood tears.
Minds lock at the monument and limbs freeze in side streets.
Cobbles trap daisies and heavy clouds drown the causeway.
For miles the darkened roads carry time in catacombs
and the couple murdered in a car, a friend murdered walking
home lie in the heat of blood and the stench of wolves.
Beautiful stars in eyes fading spangle the ground
caught like butterflies in blood from the cow's throat.
There are places here should feel like home but darkness kills
and hysterical weeping in the hall of frosty air rings.
There is little wanted but left alone with loving kisses
and the children beckoning with arms a full-blown welcoming.
On the Falls stones weep, on the Shankill stones weep
and everywhere about us eyes turned - killer never sleep.

The Hidden Curriculum

Kids curse their way to school from down-town streets,
break bus windows with Doc Martin's nervy feet.
Bakes like hatchets rankle with the driver;
teeth spit words steeled with manly rancour.
And I'm not to worry, be happy on my chair,
when the blank-faced boy in the back row
seat, crushes a flea to death there.

Under the Bridge

The Waterworks opens and shuts like clockwork.
Over the man-made islands swans and ducks glide
where the rippling lake overlooks the city.
To the basalt north Napoleon's nose lies;
to the south Goliath on greasy wheels slides.
There's a frosty sky and the north star twinkles
above the humped-backed bridge as my daughter and I
cycle nervously past boys sucking bags from the sky.
In the past people walking paid their half-a-crown for the
privilege of the paths, the privacy, the ponds.
Tonight the dusky air reels with maddening cries
and the ugly Troll under the bridge is pissed as a newt,
high on glue, wears a Cliftonville scarf
and stuffs his mouth with Manny's French fries.

The Reservation

When we left the half-moon scrubbed at our door
and moved to the new estate where we kept coal
in the bath and our fleay Fenian mongrel
scittered lino threw on the floor;

as the noose tightened, squeezing lobes,
killing the larynx; I also believed their lies!

Marriage
for Pat, Ard, Eoin and Grainne

Tonight you are gone. The late forecast tells of
storms, storms and thunder towards Holland where tomorrow
you'll be witness at an old friend's wedding.

At home the cold tap drips, sounds to kill your mood,
and our son is in bed, Amsterdam fills his head.

But each word jars; tonight I saw moths, their wings visible
through opaque glass, their dance a perfect dusty dance of stars.

Plus ça change! In a photo under deadly headlines, John
Turnley's Japanese wife sits with her son on her husband's knee.

John is dead on the Antrim Coast and the Loyalist bullets
have shattered 'a jumble of opposites knit in perfect harmony.'

And yesterday piles back in a glossy guide of Holland showing
families in perfect ease, tourists drinking at the city square;

and, on a clammy night in Belfast, only the gone are free
of their teeth, only the dead have rights to their bones.

In Queen Mary's Gardens

Against the full moon his legs straddle the gates
of Queen Mary's Gardens. The laurels are still
in bloom and the river of tins tinkles endlessly.
A Dowling painting, his big feet and matching ears
are full of the night's traffic. Roofs are shining
slate and in the distance an army helicopter sits
motionless over the old man's eye. There will be
time to drink, to love, to die, for tonight is Friday!
One hundred cans, two hundred fags, three hundred
plastic bags of genocide where the swans arrow the lake.
The boys are meditating on flags inside the railings
of Queen Mary's Gardens and under the steel Autumn Sky.
Ranged like cowboys round cards on the ground,
their lips playing with deadly crafty sounds.

Mother

At night when the Lagan like a snake poisons land,
I dream this cameo to suffer endless morn.

Mother in pink floral dress, arms folded, statue-still
near the Protestant church in balmy Ligoniel,
her blond hair flaxen free as Helens,
a sadness at the turn of her lip the only sign
of longing free from that time and place,
as she stared, hand on hip, far away over hazy
Belfast to steamers hooting their way to England
or France and the fear of father's wartime absence.
Relaxing from chores near three boys standing, two girls
drawing; a gentle gracious still from another lovely morning.

Shooting Stars at Ben Whisken

Praying for ease beside the Atlantic, my pine
door moves with the wind from the chimney.
Through the pink curtains Sligo Town in the
south ambers mountains behind Ben Whisken.
My mind deceives, deceives and calls, sees the
plough tire of stars in their flashing freefall.
Dead father's figure stoops at my bed while my
son's restless tossing troubles joists overhead.
Between the burning liver and the need for peace
facts of copulation tease tired body to its knees.
Faces come and go and the whiskied breath-like
vinegar troubles my face on the crumpled pillow.
And outside the window, blue stones on the roads
grow and grow, shadow my fear and my bitter love.

A Small Peace

1

At the red light she jerked her dog to a sudden halt.
From behind they looked like an act from a circus clown.
Her black hair wild on a too-large windy head,
her teeth smiling simply near the army siren.
A small peace, full of the wind, the sky, the strong lead;
her whole midget being in a nightmare living; our peace is safe.

2

Ascending, every square inch of varnish in the lift of the
central public library scraped and scored with graffiti.
Are the words wood or is the wood words?
I see a tree, a boat sailing, the start of a poem.
The lift stops; I have arrived too soon at where I was going.

The Cooler

Between the graveyard and the pool,
railings are bent, bent or down.
Rented-eyed boys sit on tombstones,
drink and sniff, sniff and drink.
Cars' lights on the motorway glint off marble
and above the beams sky never sleeps.
Dead dreams are here where the river
flows past swamps and factories and
the rushing blood keeps the mind dizzy.
In the pool slowly moving beyond charred trees,
a car floats in the city's deathly breeze.
Staggering over stones boys see the reeling
mountain, feel the taste of dog shit in their bones.
If this is home between falling flesh at the door and
the murdered look on the street, breath tears lungs.
And rented-boys drink and sniff, sniff and drink,
see clouds denounce sky and roll downhill
past the gates of the barracks, the grey walls
shivering under the siren's shrill night call.

Our Day Will Come

'Our day will come', comes and goes round galvanised metal.
A boy rolls snowballs adding glass for comfort, and a
dog with a shade round its neck eats Winter roses.
Rushes standing and falling breathe the wind's intention
and a swan with an arrow in its neck drifts in the lake.
Above the flood of white and under the fading blue,
ants work downhill and worms warm their feet.
A woman and man argue; he is full of blackmail
and Christ below his ear reflects the Winter night.
Someone is playing music; the notes on the wall of the
football ground encircle barbed wire, rise upward
and follow restless drunks on their daily round.
Snow falls again, blows against slogans aimed at
'British Justice', and the boy with the snowball aims his
arm at the dog with the shade and yells and yells.

Echoes

Echoes from the bomb stir turds in sewers and ruffle swans.
From the caves in the mountain to the gaps in the city,
resonance is felt in windows, ceilings and lovers sleeping.
Swallows rise like clouds of smoke and settle in eves trembling.
Like the note from a tenor, the echo is humming through
the red streets and entries, the bells in the belfries,
curling back over ghosts of the dead dreaming, where
swans and ducks shake feathers in icy islands,
and monkeys in the zoo fall back on dreams of fleas biting.

Sean O'Riada in Belfast

He stood under elms dripping and peered intently.
'Come and join us,' he said, repeating my friend's invite.
Armagh pipers had played when Queens made their award
and my player-friend Dara tugged my coat at me making a fuss.
The last I saw of O'Riada was his small figure in the clammy street
waving a friend's goodbye and me, as usual, miscreant,
wanting to tell how Mise Eire set feet tapping in a Sandy Row
shoeshop on the eleventh of July, and how customers who wouldn't
buy socks with green in them, remarked on water dripping and
clouds drifting westwards as they sailed the Irish Sea from
parts of Scotland, and how the Plymouth Brethren owner rushed
upstairs to turn the record when the music was over.
Years later I stood at the place of reverence gone and saw his
wattle moustache dripping, urging the Plymouth Band on and on.

Quilting for Ballintrillick
for Sara Raymond

Like putting a shirt on inside out and leaving it for fear
of good luck running down the arms or over the head, she has
the sky, the sea, the flowers, her tidy world from San Paolo
to the wildnesses of Ben Bulben or monbretia near the mountain.
There is a Sawtooth Border ten miles from the real one and the
machine's needle joins lattice strips and material scraps of
blouses, dresses, shirts, the design evolving as she goes along.
The weeping stone above the arched fireplace drips the face of
Christ and the settle bed is still with the last dead man in it.
Sharman's March blocks join with Lattice Straps and a
Friendship Star in greens and blues and browns at the corners.
The wind outside in the gorse, the honeysuckle and violets
are bound by the square pattern in relief, and birds in Summer
step across the binding edges under the sky and above the peat.
And all the time Monique and Leonard, Ibis and Lars Laugh,
their voices ditch-quilted like primroses under firs,
coming up from down under like a thousand others repeating the
pattern of the grey stones, the ticking meter, the open hearth,
welcoming as the central rust patches and white for outer walls.
And all the time she makes the outer inner like times from both
sides of the brain; my artist friend capturing the world again.

Pecking Order

The boys are at the crossroads playing football,
yelling and whooping, 'Pass it Joe', and 'Ah fuck me!'
Their goals are the gnarled trunks of chestnut trees.
I toot the horn, slow down to pass, and, in our leafy
suburb one youngster gives me fingers on route to Mass.
Should I turn the car, drive back home and phone police?
They are breaking the law playing on the public street.
But the boy's gesture, his resentful, too-young face
could magnify with stones, bombs, or, his father's feet.
I slow the car carefully, move into sated Knutsford Drive
where the limes have made a canopy of leaves, and what do I see?
A mallard duck leading its young from the murky Waterworks,
their bandy walk on the dusty road a Walt Disney film,
their silent pecking order heading for the boy's loud jeers.

Under the Glare of Blue

By the road to the border, police are meeting soldiers
with backpacks and guns after the recent disorder.
On the radio the three o'clock news tells of another crater
and two policemen crawling from their upturned car,
its reinforced metal bent and mangled saved their lives.
Under the glare of blue the trees in Winter silence as
I drive towards Annaghmakerrig by the lake, and,
in the last dull town north of the border, I am
stopped by two squadies in the middle of the road.
Beyond them fields and trees stretch into the Republic,
beyond the drumlins and church and overgrown mansion.
One asks for my licence and the other tells the car's
number into the mouthpiece underneath his green collar.
How quick to hear my name, the make and colour of the car
radioed back as the other tells me to open the boot.
I get out, and, for safety sake, stand at the back
as he rummages through my bag, my shoes, my books.
There is nothing said until he sees Lorca's 'New York Poems'
which he lifts, looks and says, 'The revolutionary Spanish poet!'
I don't reply, what could I say, watch helicopters in the sky,
his words surprising, his silence at mine menacing,
and blandly adds, 'Lo tiraran al jodido rulo!'
and blandly adds, 'O.K. Sir; you're clear; on you go.'

Walking the Dog

The lake is in November stillness,
swans ripple the cold glassy blue;
a dog sits still against the wall of a bridge
and plastic bags kill the blackthorn's view.
Pigeons arc like V's in the air and
boys aim stones at ducks in the lake;
Cavehill to the north is capped with clouds
and drunks on the verge are on the make.
My dog pulls tight past a woman walking,
her smile all teeth in the shadowed light.
I put one foot in front of the other,
read words of hatred scrawled in the night;
watch four schoolboys chased down the road,
their feet echoing with 'Kill the Fenian B's';
their cursing and yelling rising upward,
past the barracks and the spectral trees.

Gortnahowla

On harvest Monday I backed away from the rick
winding a shaped wire through a worn spool,
the sugan fed by the knowing hands of my neighbour,
stumbled back and fell into Gortnahowla clachan,
its orchard long decayed, its wood spoiled and torn
for fences and fires in far away places.
Sitting upright, I eyed remains of the village falling
downhill where an iron pen marked its extremity.
If you walked the field, trod tractor and hoof marks,
or climbed the largest rock for a simple aerial view, you
would discern the plan for twenty homes in their topography.
Gortnahowla upper and lower clachans touched
at the glen where the Mass Rock stood.

Summer Evening in the Gaeltacht

Tent up; one last look and downhill into Leos.
Bar is empty and Clannad's records brighten the dull walls.
My son and I among friends and the owner's face welcoming.
Hours pass quickly with a session swinging and visitors
from Germany playing tunes from the Berlin Orchestra.
Around midnight we leave; stars sparkle the velvet sky
and with my son tired on my arm we head for the Gaeltacht
where, we are assured, an oichearna is in progress.
When we arrive at the teachers' house, fuchsia bleed
at the whitewashed wall in the car's headlights.
My friend enters and quickly exits with the news.
My son and I can't speak Irish so we can't go in.
A dark figure comes after him; it is the Cardinal of
Ireland out to placate us with talk about writers and music.
Disappointed but not surprised, I reverse the car past
the empty Germans' bus, pass teachers's cars from Belfast,
Dundalk and distant parts of the east, pass a local
who, knowing me, waves and yells, 'Come over tomorrow,'
his silhouette against the rising sun from the hills,
his voice ringing over stones like welcoming bells.

Belfast Wakes

Belfast wakes with frogs on the doorstep
and cats' eyes floating yellow on saucers.
A rat squints from a dog's tail and
swallows flit drunk from presbyteries.
The Lagan drips tins through taps in kitchens
and mice weave counterpanes dreaming.
A ship sits in the old man's brain as
he eats porridge with acetylene burners.
Across the table his son devours the other side
with drills and knees and the broken tide.
Postman's feet drum in the silence as his
head turns full circle passing glassy entries.
A boy kicks bottles with nine on his brow,
mullet at the weir and skips his world of streets;
goes to the shop at the corner, slippery fingers
under the counter, and, for teachers, poisons sweets.

In Monaghan

Who says that painters can't theorise?

In the house among the drumlins
and before the freezing lake,
I stand in the dining room
and stretch my frozen bake.

At the far side of a table
a painter watches my performance.

'Monaghan,' emphasising Mon, 'is centuries old.
The damp and smell are all around us,
the floors and walls are wet and cold!'

I look at him in mild amusement,
watch his lips puck and spit.

'It's in our clothes, our ears, our beards;
even glasses in pubs smell of cow shit!'

Annacuna
for Francis Crean

Dear Anna crying, the night the stranger stood in your midst,
you took your husband's hand and left the gathering, crossed
the marshy land at the sharp incline to the mountain, felt
the speckled stones slipping downhill as you made your way
up the side of the waterfall to the gap in Skib where you
lay on the dewy sprit and, under the frosty sky, felt the baby
moving, your man beside you whispering comfort as you pushed
and pushed, stifling your cries, until your daughter lay
bloodied on the hasty rug of your petticoats flung awry.
And when she cried, you heard the sound of hooves under you
as your husband crept to the edge and saw soldiers dismount,
and slaughter neighbours from the lowlands about who had been
incautious to their former troubles and languished merry in
child-like simplicity, thinking they were safe in the booley.
You had tried to warn of peril, but they took no heed, and
your daughter's crying was almost choked to death by the grasp
to your breast, and the yells for mercy stabbing hills as
the soldiers had their way and left all dead including their
prisoner who had led them from their home in Manorhamilton.
Years later with Una Strong, you went to the waterfall and
lay on the Monrock to rest but fell asleep that night and slept
too long, cursed the rushes at the burial place until their
hearts withered and died, useless for roofing or making light..

My Daughter Asleep

The abacus is put away. Under a festive eiderdown,
my daughter's fair curls spill on her cheeks
and cover the face of the circus clown.
She breathes to the tune of Jack and Jill
as they link each other from hill to hill.
Her fingers entwine hair while a white silken
scarf comfort neck and breast there.
Above her head the brass bed rises through
daisychains and ribbons where an Eastern idol
with outspread wings and jewelled eyes
bends from the mantelpiece and staves
safe the night with blessed caring sighs.

The Strangest Angle

1

A willie-wag-tail pecks at crumbs
dropped from the schoolboy's lunch,

makes a sudden lively shock
when wind blows a sweetie box;

hops to a puddle, sees the trees
and sky from the strangest angle,

and with no visible means of support
dodges the path of a looming blackbird.

2

In the classroom boys are full of restless
humour, dreaming of the warmth of bed,

climbing roofs near the River Lagan
and buying glue from the weight of lead.

Maisonette Madonna
for Brendan Ellis

>*So there you sit. And how much blood was shed*
>*That you might sit there. Do such stories bore you?*
>Bertholt Brecht

My maisonette madonna,
the ragged child at your breast,
clings tight and drags you down,
down past your varicose veins
to the mongrel dog on the ground.

You hold him tight and sigh,
sigh past the balcony,
the foot-patrol on the road
and the bitter yells of children
under this never-open sky.

Tobernalt

Here the silence fills, whorls me still in time and space.

Debris and bins from Garland Sunday stretch from tree to tree
and litter the Holy Well. A car revs where waves lap a pier,
each yellow top tugs at the memory.

But what time and what space?

I see them come by foot, by boat, their silent faith like
the jutting granite outgrowth, the hills leafed by a larch-
filled sky, the top shelf to view lake and road nearby.

But what time and what space?

Eyes tight I hear the muffled chaunt. Prayers are blown
from the mud-caked path past chalice and priest, whisked
over air and moor to the garrison's rampart.

But what time and what space?

A cup hangs from the well's wall. Many have drank here
and even on the warmest day water, cool and steady in its flow,
pumps deep and free in this time, space, I still don't know.

Both Taig an Prod

You see Sir, it happened like this. Me and Pamela my girl were sitting at the end of Delhi Street talkin about things. Two mates came along talkin about futbal and stuff, and all of a sudden it turned til religion. I felt out of it bein both Taig an Prod, me ma an da mixed in marriage ye see. So I says til Pamela, 'I'm away on home luv.' I thought I'd cross the Ormeau Bridge and pik a fight with me mate John over there. You see Sir, I had til take it out on someone. When I got halfway across I changed me mind. I sat on the wall of the bridge, me legs hanging over the black water in the Lagin, when all of a suddin I see the police an army coming towards me there. One yelled, 'Don't jump son; take it aisy' and another tuk his coat aff. At this point I fell, a black shape in after me. The water was freezing an all. I don't remember nathing, just the ambulance an police pullin me over the hard wall. Thank Christ they were around; I niver thought I'd say this, cause if me mates heard me, they'd have bate me inta the groun.

Driving the Roads of Sligo

Driving the roads of Sligo, the wet black roads of Sligo,
a starling and leaves partner wipers and slide down the window.
Evenings are closing in and darkness in the valleys and fields
murders the end of Autumn and grips the mind like a migraine.
Water arrows from tyres and the car floats like a waterbed.
Behind trees lights disappear and everywhere the cemetery.
Few on the road to brave the night flap like scarecrows.
Water spills downhill and the fall in the windy gap is flung
upward, its head a spray of light on Finn's darkened crag.
Come my love and lie in this land of wetness and weep.
The dark is in my skull and my eyes and my sleep.
The car's radio the only solace playing Polish music and my
passenger, my Champion guy-of-nee-chek in the driver's seat,
the meagre soup on the ground, a needle of phenol at his feet.

With Hearts Cut Out

Far below the road, deep below the blue,
grey oaks shuddered over moss-coloured stones.

At a lane's end, water edged past the Falls Road
Workhouse, the new home for villains and orphans.

Before they built the new estate, boys came here for
mitching and stealing or the sins their elders enjoyed.

Under eyes of La Salle Brothers, young offenders passed
the park and cemetery to queue at the cinema's entrance.

One Saturday the balcony hummed. Down below the boys sat in
rows to watch in silent homage where cowboys fought and roamed.

When it ended, they walked in twos along the silent pavement,
round the bend past the lane to duck's nests in bog meadows;

past holy pictures, down bare stairs to toilets of stench,
where booths with hearts cut out viewed each cold bench.

Ramblers

On Bulben we plod from tussock
and drain to the mountain's edge.
The beach below our feet turns
like a new moon, and roads to the north
are ribbons glinting in a toy hedge.
The wind cools back across the moor
where figures are monochromed in bog,
and a partridge flies off, its beat
heading into the dusky sight, the
sucking moors disappearing with
its swerving jittery flight.

Joy-Riders

He lay in the car with bullets in his chest.
Paras didn't know him not knowing himself.

How grass shivered through broken glass!

It was dark when they looked in
and shone lights round the bloodied car.
The girl huddled with pain and fear
knew it was the end of her.

What a way to end joy!
What a way to silence wind
in the grass and leaves shivering.

How trees wept through broken glass!

Paras didn't dare to open eyes or tell guns
how the darkness shivered under the mountain.
And silence in beams on the hedge shattered
when they looked through glass glinting
under lamps in the steely-wet road-night,
their hearts in darkened faces eating bullets
like men hoarding gold in cities of fright.

Ritual
November 1975

Tonight a single shot fractured Autumn's air.
I didn't care, went on eating, talked with wife and
cherub-faced heir about paintings and the new car.

Minutes later, yards away, halted by a cop who leered
and said, 'Can't go past; got one in the belly; Dead!'
And me unsure at first asking which way was safe,
past the charred bus, up the lampless street?

Not feeling pain, the sixteen year-old pain as
he clutched an imitation gun a Godfather made
years ago, moaned in the dark 'Help me! Help me!'

Would the sky could crack and swallow sooth that
sordid frightening scene as sirens screeched through
night air where we stay born, bred, weaned.

Tooneenvalley
for Nancy, Matt and Zach across 'The Abyss of Tears'.

Between the loaded fuchsia and the broken fir,
the moon rides where the road meets hedges.
Fields carry the mountain and brace Atlantic
and time is laid to rest in flooded meadows.
There is no time for cowards and the shuffling badger
yearns for wheels of cars in silent badgers' corner.
Below the clasai snow is heaped on snow and
my love lies there with charcoal in her mouth.
Let water turn to mist and teach me to persist
like the mad blind poet with pots on his bag
and holes for seeing in his happy wrinkled eyes.
Or my blind pet seal under the table lifting his
head sniffing air and going under before storm;
his comic flesh moving from the lighted lantern.

The Sonorous Streets

The sonorous streets; in the beginning
wise men came to study them.
Faces and bricks were possibilities,
commodes and catheters openings.

Rain poured from Black Mountain,
cascaded green stones of the cathedral and
backyard toilets opened like confessions.

All was objective, brisk, as rain teemed
and soldiers frisked the old on route from jail.
Nothing was hidden: pain, laughter, horror.
Every bit was measured and the worst stressed.
Everyone who touched ground was left witless.

At the end the three stood silent;
one had mummerings of fear in him and faces
and bricks were more solemn than ever.

Wise men closed books and left; their
presents were maps drawn on the page.
Rain poured from Black Mountain, its song, a song
of death in washed-out tricky pavements.

Not Today Son, Not Today

Sunday Morning. A long blue light spreading west.
After Mass, my son and I eager to feed swans,
the lower lake chopped by a raw wind
from brooding Cavehill.

A frothy scum whipped to the lake's edge.
Each roofless shelter built for pensioners daubed
'H Block' 'Dawsy Rules' 'God Bless Are Queen
and Are Ulster' aerosoled on bench and wall.

Swans honking, beating the March air,
rising in groups to circle The New Lodge
where beer tins, papers, crowd the grassy verge.
'Looks like we'll have to wait,' I said,

when the child's eyes asked, 'What is it dad?'
Down and wings, a sogged soaking mass like
mother soaking sheepskin in the bath,
the beak twisted underneath,

the limp neck an inverted 'V' at the break.
And again, 'What is it dad? Is it sick?'
The light fading at our feet.
'Not today son, not today!'